Thomas Richey

The Question of the Day

What is the Bible, for what Object was it written, and how it is to be read

Thomas Richey

The Question of the Day
What is the Bible, for what Object was It written, and how it is to be read

ISBN/EAN: 9783337172848

Printed in Europe, USA, Canada, Australia, Japan

Cover: Foto ©ninafisch / pixelio.de

More available books at **www.hansebooks.com**

THE QUESTION OF THE DAY

WHAT IS THE BIBLE

FOR WHAT OBJECT WAS IT WRITTEN

AND

HOW IT IS TO BE READ

BY

THOMAS RICHEY, D.D.

PROFESSOR OF ECCLESIASTICAL HISTORY, GENERAL THEOLOGICAL SEMINARY

––––––––

NEW YORK

JAMES POTT, CHURCH PUBLISHER

12 ASTOR PLACE

1883

I.

WHAT IS THE BIBLE?

I.

WHAT IS THE BIBLE?

THE Bible, as the title indicates, is the book of books. Most true! And yet the answer is not altogether satisfactory. Its superiority granted, the question still remains, How does the Bible differ from all other books? And to this it is not enough to say, the Bible is a revelation of God from heaven. For Nature, too, is God's book. How, then, we are constrained to ask, does the revelation of God in the Bible differ from the revelation which God makes of Himself in the book of Nature? To this the Bible itself furnishes, I think, a satisfactory answer (Ps. xix),—

7

" The heavens are declaring the glory of God,
    and the firmament is shewing His handy-
        work ;
day to day poureth forth speech,
    and night to night breatheth forth knowledge,
no speech is there, there are no words,
    all inaudible is their voice :—
their line goeth forth into all lands,
    and their signs to the world's end,
where He has fixed for the sun a tent :
    And He steppeth forth as a bridegroom from His
        chamber,
    and rejoiceth as a mighty man to run His
        course ;
from the uttermost part of the heaven He has His
    rising,
    and His circuit to the end of it again ;
and there is nothing hid from the heat thereof."

From this manifestation of God in Nature, (where it will be observed the name of God—Êl—occurs only *once*), the Psalmist passes on in the second part of the Psalm to praise God for His more perfect revelation of Himself in the Law :—

" The law of the Lord is perfect—restoring the soul ;
> the testimony of the Lord is faithful—making wise
>> the simple :
the precepts of the Lord are right—rejoicing the heart ;
> the commandment of the Lord is pure—enlight-
>> ening the eyes:
the fear of the Lord is clean—enduring forever ;
> the judgments of the Lord are truth—they are
>> righteous altogether :
More to be desired are they than gold or much fine gold ;
> and sweeter than honey, or the droppings of the
>> comb :
moreover by them is Thy servant warned ;
> in keeping them there is great reward."

Here, it will be noted, the name YAHVEH occurs *seven* times ; the number and the change of name indicating that it is no longer God as the Divine Governor of the world which is the subject of consideration, but the Covenant God of Israel in His special work of Redemption.

It is beyond all question, then, that the Bible at the first was given to the Jews, and was placed as a precious deposit in their keep-

1*

ing.   It is also beyond all question that the New Testament Scriptures were written more especially for the Christian Church, and together with the Old were handed down by it from generation to generation.   It is also beyond all question that both the Jewish and the Christian Churches were of the opinion that in the Scriptures so handed down they had a certified record of God's dealings with the Church and people from the beginning to the end of time, and were accustomed to have recourse to the Bible accordingly.* These are the simple facts of the case.   Now let us see what may fairly be deduced from them.   It is clear then, as a matter of fact, that the

---

* For what is the *matter* of the Bible but those acts and words of God in which He has opened His very heart, and disclosed to us His purposes of salvation—that whole great, glorious history in which His thoughts of love have been revealed and fulfilled? For the Bible is no mere collection of maxims, and precepts, or religious truths, but that great history of salvation which, commencing with the first beginning of the race, was continued through the times of the patriarchs and prophets, culminated in Jesus Christ and the events of His death and resurrection, and will be completed in that future world which is promised to us."—Luthardt.

Bible, at the first, was not given into the possession of the world at large, but was intended for the exclusive use of a peculiar
people. Whether or not this was to be the
case for all time is another question; and
has nothing to do with the facts of the case
as they present themselves before us just
now for consideration. The Bible, it is to be
feared, has suffered as much from the un-
warranted claims put forth for it by its
friends as it has from the slights which from
time to time are attempted to be put upon
it by its enemies. When it is claimed, for
example, that, because the Bible is from
God, it must be intended to teach everybody
everything—this is to put abstract speculation
in the place of historical fact, and to ignore
the limitations which the distinctive character
of the revelation of necessity imposes upon
it. It is just as bad to make too much of the
Bible as it is to make too little of it. The
Bible is not an encyclopedia of universal

knowledge, nor was it ever intended to be. It is true that the Bible is a revelation from heaven ; but it is not true that it is the only revelation from heaven. God reveals Himself, as has been said, in one way in Nature and the Conscience : in another way, in the Bible and the Church. The Bible does not take the place of the Conscience : it corrects, it may be, and supplements it : nor does the Church, to whose existence from the beginning the Bible bears testimony, take the place of Nature, and the powers to whom God has given authority therein. Here, as elsewhere, we have the testimony, not of one, but of two or three witnesses.*

Again, there are people who will insist upon

* " When we extol the complete sufficiency of the entire body of the Scripture," says Hooker, "it must be understood with this caution, that the benefit of nature's light be not thought excluded as unnecessary, because the necessity of a diviner light is magnified. It sufficeth, therefore, that Nature and Scripture do serve in such full sort that they both conjointly and not severally either of them be so complete, that unto everlasting felicity we need not the knowledge of anything more than these two may easily furnish our minds with on all sides."

going to the Bible with all manner of hard questions, and are disappointed if they do not find the solution of their questions there. Now this again is to expect more from the Bible than it was ever intended to fulfill. The Bible addresses itself primarily to faith, not to reason. It does not solve hard questions, for the reason that the people for whom it was more especially written are not of the kind supposed to entertain such questions. If people will have their doubts and difficulties set at rest, they must go elsewhere than to the Bible. The Bible is the certified record of God's dealings with His Church and people. It was written accordingly for the instruction and education of faith, not to answer hard questions. The case of Pharaoh, over which people sometimes puzzle themselves, is a case in point. It is something for faith to know that the evil as well as the good is in the hands of God. Evil angels and bad men, while permitted to do harm and work mischief for a time, will in the end be made to do God's bidding.   As to the Ethical questions involved, the Bible itself gives no answer to them.   It is the function of Philosophy to reconcile the sovereignty of God with the free agency of man, not of a guide to faith and a book written for the edification of God's own Church and people.   If people *will* insist upon an answer to their questions, and will find fault with the Bible for not furnishing them with what they ask, they are simply unreasonable and their extravagance is not to be charged as a fault to the disparaging of a book expressly written, as has been said, to aid faith, and not to gratify reason.

Then there are a class of people who find fault with the Bible because it does not speak in technical language, and is in manifest contradiction to the discoveries of science, they say.   They might just as well find fault with the world they live in, and

criticise the way God has chosen to reveal
Himself in nature. The world, as it appears
to us to be, is in flat contradiction to the world
which men of science will insist upon our
thinking it to be. We talk of the sun's rising
and setting, notwithstanding it is not the
sun which moves around the earth, but it is
the earth which moves round the sun.
Strange to say, men of science every day use
language which they themselves declare is in
open contradiction to what they know and
teach. But what if the phenomenal world
has its own story to tell as well as the
maze of fixed laws in which science delights
to revel? The fair beauty of the world,
as reflected in sun, moon and stars, and
painted by the Divine Artist in glory upon
the sky, it is to be believed, has its
own mission, and is not altogether without a purpose. May it not be that to the
great mass of men, the beauty of nature as
seen by the eye, or as distilled by music into

the ear, has an evidential value quite as
powerful in its way as the order of nature and the hidden harmony of its laws?
May it not be that the emotions kindled in
the heart of the savage, as he stands awe-
stricken in the presence of the Power which
speaks to him in the voice of the thunder
or the roar of the ocean, are of equal
moral and spiritual value with the intellect-
ual pleasure which fills the mind of the
scientist when he contemplates the order
and arrangement which pervade the whole
system of nature? What if the belief which
rises spontaneously at the sight of the
beauty of the world, and breaks out in
hymns of adoring gratitude and songs of
unending praise be intended to counter-
work the unbelief which the spirit of inquiry
fosters, and the doubts* suggested by the

* See Canon Mosley's sermon upon "Nature": "It is thus that
the admiration of the beauty of nature strikes a sort of balance
with the scientific analysis of nature in the general effect upon
the religious mind of an age. The tendency of the analysis of

development of the critical faculties. Be
this as it may, the Bible follows the course
of nature in speaking to man through the
medium of phenomenal and every-day language, and does not make use of exact or
of scientific speech. Nay, more, as it was
the calling of the Jew to keep alive in the
world the knowledge of the one living and
true God in opposition to the idolatry of the
powers of nature, the Bible always and every-

nature is to reduce the idea of the Deity in men's minds to a nega-
tion, and to convert the First Great Cause into a mere physical
force. But the admiration of nature as a creation of beauty, on
the other hand, tends to support the moral idea of the Deity, to
excite a curiosity and interest about His character, and so far to
sustain the mystery of the Gospel disclosure of His character.
One and the same age has developed in a signal manner both of
these principles ; two influences have gone forth from it, and the
physical idea of nature from analysis, and the mystical and imag-
inative idea from the picture have contended within its bosom,
and sometimes within the same minds. The impression from the
visible world, as a chain of material causation, has been more or
less counteracted and counterbalanced by the visible world as a
spiritual sight. A spiritual fact ever before us is a spiritual me-
mento; and beauty is a spiritual fact, because it altogether hinges
upon a spiritual principle within us, and only exists as an address
to it. And so we generally find that no one set of ideas is allowed to domineer and monopolize ground in any age, but, when
one rises to power, another is provided to meet and check it."

where speaks of God as present and acting, without regard to the laws of nature, or the teachings of science. It is for Reason to discover the ways of God in nature and history; it is for Faith to trace the dealings of God with His own elect Church and people. The one is not in opposition to the other any more than it is to pray to God as the Giver and Bestower of all things, to "give us this day our daily bread," while we bend ourselves, notwithstanding, to toil, knowing that if a man will not labor he has no right to expect to eat. Faith views the world on its supernatural side; science, on its natural side; sight, on its phenomenal side. There is a language of faith, just as there is a language of science; and there is a common speech which interprets the world as mere phenomena. The truth of the language in every case depends upon the point of view from which, at the time of speaking or writing, we are looking at the world and all that is therein. Between the different points of view there is no necessary contradiction. There *is* no contradiction, except when fools and pedants will insist upon it that their own point of view is the only point of view, and will compel everybody to look at things through their spectacles. Men of science in this respect have been as much at fault as theologians; and worse than all is the irrational crowd which will believe nothing except what it sees with its eyes. There is no real conflict to-day—there never has been any—between the Bible and science; between the natural and the supernatural; between faith and reason. The conflict, if there be any, is between belief and unbelief; and when it reaches that point, neither the revelation of God in nature, nor the revelation of God in the Bible, is of any avail to convince the gainsayer.*

* "The question concerning the origin of matter, leaving the region of sensible reality, passes into that of speculation or of faith. At this point, then, natural science ceases to be natural science, and

It is a matter of complaint on the part of purists, as well as of those who affect a high tone in morals, that there are things in the Bible which are not to be found in ordinary books upon moral culture. Possibly! The Bible deals with moral science, just as it deals with physical science. It does not treat of the science of Ethics, but has to do with the facts on which morals as a science rest; its arrangement is not scientific but historical; not formal, but economical. It was necessary, in accordance with the plan which God in redemption had in view, that the whole mystery of sin and evil should be allowed to

becomes either philosophy or religion. Whether we admit matter to have been created by God, or look upon it as self-existent and eternal, or whether we do not concern ourselves with it at all, is a matter of equal indifference as far as natural science, which starts from the existence of material being, is concerned. Hence, in this question, there neither is nor can be any conflict between science and faith. If a conflict does take place, it is one between two opposite views of the world, which are both as views originally accepted from other sources. Matters of faith, whether that faith be a religious or a philosophical one; what seem at first a conflict with science, is rather a conflict with the philosophy which her votaries accept."—Luthardt.)

reveal itself, before the remedy provided
could be applied. There are ugly things in
the Bible just as there are filthy and disgust-
ing creatures in nature. There are typical
bad men in Holy Scripture just as there are
typical good men. The Bible has not only
to do with Christ, but with Ante-Christ also.
Abel has his Cain ; Jacob, his Esau ; Isaac, his
Ishmael ; Elijah, his Balaam ; David, his Saul.
The mystery of evil is permitted to reveal
itself along with the mystery of redemption.
Nor are the good men of the Bible ideal characters. They have their faults, which are, for
the most part, the exaggeration of their virtues. And their virtues, at the last, are won
by the overcoming of their faults. The
moral law, as it is revealed in the Bible, is
not an abstract code of ethics, or, as some
will have it, a re-declaration of the law of
Nature. Sin was first allowed to reveal itself ;
then the law was given to correct it. The
first commandment bears witness against

the idolatry of Israel in Egypt; the presence of which it speaks is the presence revealed in the Tabernacle, not the Great Spirit which the Indian bows down to and worships. The Sabbath is to be kept, not as a nature-festival, but as a memorial of redemption.

The Bible, then, is a book *sui generis.* It is not an encyclopedia of universal knowledge; nor is it given to serve the place of a book of puzzles; nor is it a scientific treatment of moral and physical questions. It was written for a peculiar people; it was given for a special purpose. It is but fair in judging of it, to look at it from the point of view from which the writers regard the subjects of which they treat.* The Bible is not to

---

* Although the Scripture of God, therefore, be stored with infinite variety of matter of all kinds, although it abound with all sorts of laws, yet the principal intent of Scripture is to deliver the laws of duties supernatural. . . The testimonies of God are true, the testimonies of God are perfect, the testimonies of God are all-sufficient for that end for which they were given. Therefore, accordingly, we do receive them. We do not think that in them God

be blamed for not throwing light on things with which it has nothing at all properly to do. A bird's-eye view of the contents will make all this abundantly plain. Take, first of all, the Pentateuch, or five books of Moses. "The entire work," says Professor Kiel, "though divided into five parts, forms, both in plan and execution, one complete and carefully contrasted whole, commencing with the creation, and reaching to the death of Moses, the mediator of the old covenant. The foundation for the Divine plan was really laid in and along with the creation of the world. The world which God created is the scene of a history embracing both God and man, the site for the kingdom of God in its temporal and earthly form. All that the *first* book contains with reference to the early

hath omitted anything needful to His purpose, and left His intent to be accomplished by our devisings. What the Scripture purposeth, the same in all points it doth perform. Howbeit that we swerve not in judgment, one thing especially we must observe, namely, that the absolute perfection of Scripture is seen by relation to that end whereto it tendeth."—Hooker.

history of the human race, from Adam to the patriarchs of Israel, stands in a more or less relation to the kingdom of God in Israel, of which the other books describe the actual establishment. The *second* depicts the inauguration of the kingdom of Sinai. Of the *third* and *fourth*, the former narrates the spiritual, the latter the political organization of the kingdom of God by facts and moral precepts. The *fifth* recapitulates the whole in a hortatory strain, embracing both history and legislation, and impresses it upon the hearts of the people, for the purpose of arousing true fidelity to the covenant, and securing its lasting duration." It is a puzzle to many readers of the Bible why the books which contain the further history of the people of God from the death of Moses to the Babylonish captivity, viz., Joshua, Judges, 1 and 2 Samuel, 1 and 2 Kings, are reckoned among the prophetical books. The Jews called these books the *Prophetae priores.*

They did so because the period covered by
these books is regarded not from an historical, but from a prophetical point of
view. The writers treat the subject not
after the manner of annalists, but with a view
to the instruction and edification of the
Church. It is the prophetical element, as in
the review which Moses makes of the early
history of God's people in the book of Deuter-
onomy, which is of real value in these historical books, not the order of events regarded as
mere facts of history. So also with the later
prophets (*prophetae posteriores*) Isaiah, Jeremiah, Ezekiel, the twelve minor prophets;
they are not mere predictions of future
events, but "contain the progressive testimony to the council of God, delivered in
connection with the acts of God, during the
gradual decay of the Old Testament kingdom." It is, again, a puzzle to many why
the Book of Ruth in the Jewish arrangement
of the Canon should be torn away from its

2

historical relationship as an appendix to the Book of Judges, and placed among the Hagiographa or holy writings with the Song of Solomon and the Lamentations of Jeremiah. But the answer is not hard to find.   It is the mystical element in the book, connected with the introduction of a Moabitess into the Church and kingdom of God which gives it its place in the Canon of Scripture. Nothing could be further from the spirit of Jewish exclusiveness than such a thought. It looked forward to the introduction of an entire foreign element into the Church and kingdom of God which was to find its ultimate realization in the ingathering of the Gentiles. There could be no greater evidence of an overruling hand in the arrangement of the Old Testament Canon than that a book containing the evidence of such a fact should find a place in the Jewish Scriptures.   It is the same mystical element which gives to the Song of Solomon its place in the Hagiogra-

pha. It is not a mere love song, as the profane mockers of whom the Psalmist speaks
will have it to be.   The little sister of the
bride that is " black but comely," foreshadows
an alliance with the outlying world of sinners
among the Gentiles, and marks with festive
rejoicing (as the return of the prodigal in St.
Luke's Gospel in the New Testament) the
introduction of an entirely foreign element
into the Church of God.*   Men may scoff

---

* " If the Shulamite represents Israel—the typical Israel—her
sister not yet grown up can only represent that part of mankind
which is not yet fitted to undergo the trial to which this nation was
the first to be submitted,—heathen mankind, therefore. The reader
will perhaps ask himself whether the eyes of the ancient poet could
pierce so far into the future.   But does not Solomon himself, when
he is inaugurating the Temple, and dedicating that building to
Jehovah as His dwelling-place in Israel, expressly set apart a place
for the Gentiles in this House.   Does he not ask that their prayers
also may be heard ?   " Moreover, concerning a stranger, that is not
of thy people Israel, but cometh out of a far country for thy name's
sake (for they shall hear of thy great name, and of thy strong
hand, and of thy stretched out-arm); when he shall come and pray
toward this house ; hear thou in heaven, thy dwelling-place, and
do according to all that the stranger calleth to thee for : that all
people of the earth may know thy name, to fear thee, as do thy
people Israel."
  "Did not Solomon at the summit of his glory, see a representa-

at the idea of a prophet like Hosea, taking
to himself a "wife of whoredom, and children of whoredom," but their scoffing only
betrays the ignorance of what Holy Scriptures in such a case really means to teach,
and of their inability to appreciate the fore-
shadowing of the mystery of the union of
Divinity with fallen, outcast humanity in the
person of the eternal Son of God.* It is the
old Pharisaic cant about eating and drinking
with publicans and sinners. God help the
world, if it is to be given over to the tender
mercies of Puritans and unbelievers. Satan

tive of this Gentile world, a foreign queen, arrive at Jerusalem, attracted not by the fame of his name only, but also by that of the
name of Jehovah, whose appearance may well have contributed to
awaken in the poet's mind the idea of this personification of pagan
humanity in the young sister of the Shulamite? The Gentiles will
one day have to decide on their destiny, as Israel is now called to
decide on its own. They, too, will have to choose between the
visions of a false glory, and the happiness enjoyed in the love of
God ; between the Messiah crowned with gold, and the Messiah
whose hair is wet with the dews of night or even whose head is
crowned with thorns."—Godet.

* See Aubertein on Daniel and the Revelation, (p. 279) for an
admirable treatment of this whole subject.

never plays a better rôle than when he turns reformer, and affects morality.

When we turn to the New Testament, we can trace the same essential features of Divine Revelation prevailing throughout. The four Gospels are not narratives in the ordinary meaning of the word, nor are they what is commonly known as "inspired pro- ductions," as when men sit down to spin out of their own brain a book. The four Gos- pels, as Mr. Wescott in his very able intro- duction has conclusively proved, are the record of the oral teaching of the Apostles, as that teaching was arranged and modified to suit the exigencies and the varying needs of the Apostolic Church. The Gospels are not abstract and ideal productions; they grew out of the felt needs of God's people, and were arranged accordingly. St. Matthew adapted his teaching to meet the wants of the Jewish communities. St. Mark, under the guidance of St. Peter, wrote his Gospel

of the kingdom for the Romans.   St. Luke,
with St. Paul for his master, wrote to vindi-
cate the introduction of sinners into the
kingdom, and to help the Gentile churches.
St. John produced his spiritual Gospel to
meet a more advanced stage of spiritual experience ; and to bring out in connection
with it the sacramental element bound up
with the taking of humanity into union with
the Godhead in the person of Christ.   The
inspiration which arranged and adjusted the
facts of our Lord's life, and grouped and
methodized His teaching, was not a verbal
or a mechanical inspiration ; but part and
parcel of that promised gift of the Comforter,
Who, after their Lord's departure, was to
remain with the disciples and bring to
their " remembrance " all the things which
He had said unto them, as the course of
events, and the guidance of Divine Provi-
dence, and their own ordinary experience,
showed the apostles and their fellow-labor-

ers in the Lord, the things of Christ in a new light. The Holy Spirit taught them how to apply their growing experience for the edification of Christ's Church and people. There is nothing mechanical in all this; no book-making; no fine writing; but, what is better far, a Christian realism and the working of a Presence and a Power which is none other than Divine.*

* Godet (" Studies on the New Testament") puts this admirably well : Four portraits of Himself. This is the whole of the legacy left by Jesus to His family on earth. But they are sufficient for its needs, because by the contemplation of these the Church receives into herself, through the communications of the Spirit, the life of Him whose characteristic features they set forth.

These pictures originated spontaneously and (the first three, at all events) independently of each other. They arose, accidentally in a manner, from the four principal regions of the earth comprehended by the Church in the first century—Palestine, Asia Minor, Greece, Italy.

The characteristics of these four regions have not failed to exercise a certain influence upon the manner in which the Christ has been presented in the pictures intended for the use of each. In Palestine, Matthew proclaimed Jesus as Him who put the finishing-stroke to the establishing of that holy kingdom of God which had been fore-announced by the prophets, and of which the foundations had been laid in Israel. In Rome, Mark presented Him as the irresistible conqueror who founded His divine right to the possession of the world upon His miraculous power. Among the

As the Gospels do not furnish us with a detailed narrative of all the events of the

generous and affable Hellenic races, Luke described Him as the Divine philanthropist commissioned to carry out the work of divine grace and compassion toward the worst of sinners. In Asia Minor, that ancient cradle of theosophy, John pictured Him as the Word made flesh, the Eternal Life and Light, who had descended into the world of time.   Thus it was under the influence of a profound sympathy with those about him that each evangelist brought into relief that aspect of Christ which answered most nearly to the ideal of His readers.

But, on the other hand, each of the evangelists has also, by means of the picture which He has drawn, pronounced a judgmen^t upon whatever was impure in the aspirations with which, in some respects, He sympathized.   The spiritual and inspired Messianic idea presented by Matthew condemned that political and carnal view of the Church, which is the very soul of false Judaism.   The sanctified and divine Romanism of Mark condemned the Cæsarism of mere brute force.   The heavenly Atticism of Luke took the place of the frivolous and corrupt Hellenism encountered by Paul at Athens.   Lastly, humanitarianism—the divine humanitarianism of John—stands as an eternal witness against the humanitarianism, profane and anti-divine in its nature, of a world dazzled with its own greatness and lost in evil.

Our Gospels are at once magnets to draw to themselves whatever is left of divine in the depths of human nature, and, as it were, winnowing machines to lift out from it whatsoever is sinful. Hence the power both of attraction and repulsion which they exert upon the natural heart of man.

It has sometimes been asked why, instead of the four Gospels, God did not cause a single one to be written in which all the events should have been arranged in their chronological order, and the history of Jesus portrayed with the accuracy of a legal docu-

life of Christ, so in the Acts of the Apostles we have not a history of the Apostolic Church,

ment. If the drawing up of the Gospels had been the work of human skill, it would no doubt have taken this form ; but it is just here that we seem to be able to lay a finger upon the altogether Divine Nature of the impulse which originated the work.

Just as a gifted painter who wished to immortalize for a family the complete likeness of the father, who had been its glory, would avoid any attempt at combining in a single portrait the insignia of all the various offices he had filled, representing him in the same picture as a general and a magistrate, as man of science, and as father of a family, but would prefer to paint four distinct portraits, each of which should represent him in one of these characters—so has the Holy Spirit preserved for mankind the perfect likeness of Him who was its chosen representative. God in man used means to impress upon the minds of the writers whom He has made His organs four different images—the King of Israel (Matthew) ; the Saviour of the world (Luke); the Son, who as man mounts to the steps of the Divine throne (Mark); and the Son who descends into humanity to sanctify the world (John).

The single object which is represented by these four aspects of the glory of Jesus Christ could not be presented to the minds of men in a single book ; it could not be so in the form under which it was originally embodied—that of a life ; first in the Church— that body of Christ which was destined to contain and display all the fullness which dwelt in the Head ; and then again in the person of each individual believer, if that is true which Jesus said : "Ye in Me, and I in you "; and we are each of us called to make the personality of Jesus live again in ourselves in all the rich harmony of His perfection.

In the Church, then—in you, in me—we behold the living synthesis which were to be the result of that wonderful analyses of the person of Jesus Christ which produced our several Gospel narratives. The harmony of the four Gospels is something better than

2*

but an account of the planting of the Church
through the agency of the two great Apostles, St. Peter and St. Paul. The Epistles of
the New Testament are not formal treatises
on questions of doctrine and discipline, but
letters written to churches throughout the
world as the exigencies of the occasion de-
manded, and are the expression of the voice
of the Church through her recognized teach-
ers on matters appertaining to Christian
faith and practice.* The volume of reve-

the best written book ; it is the *new man* to be formed in each
believer.

* Will any one ask how such contrasts could arise among writers equally inspired ?   The question itself shows how well the idea
of inspiration has been understood in the Church, and what a
transformation it will have to undergo.   Just as the water with
which we water the seed sown in the ground does not create the
plant which grows out of it, but stimulates the development of
the organs which had been previously found in the germ, and sets
their power in action, so in the same way the Holy Spirit does not
substitute Himself for the individuality of the sacred Author.   He
awakens his faculties, He groups his experience, He places him in
immediate contact with salvation, and by that means confers upon
him a special gift—the distinct intuition of that aspect of Gospel
truth which answers most especially to his own character and
needs.   For, as M. Reuss admirably says, speaking of the differ-
ence of the sacred writers, "The pole which attracted the mag-

lation closes with the Book of the Revelation in which the future history of the Church to the end of time is disclosed, but in a way not to interfere with human liberty. The Bible, then, is no common book; it deals with no common subject. It takes for granted a Church and people of God as existing in the world from the beginning to the end of time, and reveals to us the ways of God in His relation to them. Beyond this, the Bible saith not; and no man, be he friend or enemy, has the right to quote it as an authority.

netic needle of the sentiment, or of their intelligence, was not situated for all in the same point in the sphere of revelation."— Godet.

II.

FOR WHAT OBJECT WAS THE BIBLE WRITTEN?

II.

FOR WHAT OBJECT WAS THE BIBLE WRITTEN?

O this it may be answered, the word written was never intended to take the place of the word preached. There is a Protestant Bibliolatry that is as bad in its way as Roman Mariolatry. When a man gives it as an excuse for not going to church, that he can stay at home and read his Bible, there is surely a monstrous delusion some-where. The ear as the instrument of hear-ing and obedience, not the eye, as the symbol of intelligence, is the organ of conversion. Preaching is of the very essence of Chris-

tianity.   Jesus conquers, not by the sword,
but by the Word.   His kingdom in the world
is founded not upon force, but upon moral
suasion.   He will have willing disciples
or he will have none.   His first effort ever
is to convince the reason and to enthrall the
heart.   It was for this reason that he went
up and down the length and breadth of Judea,
preaching everywhere the Gospel.   He
wrote nothing.   Himself the truth, He spoke
the truth to men, to win them to Himself, and
to make them His disciples.   He gave no
commandment to His Apostles to write. They
were to preach.   The instrument of the
spirit in working conviction in the minds and
hearts of men was to be a man, a moral
agent speaking as man to men, with authority, and filled with fire from on high.   The
Apostles were to preach, and as they preached
they were to make disciples.   It was not
themselves they preached, but Christ and
Him crucified.   It is so now.   Preaching is a

divine ordinance. Nothing—not even the Bible—can take its place, as the instrument of the world's conversion. It is grossly to abuse and not to use the Bible, to put it in the place of the living instrument which God Himself in Christ has consecrated and ordained. The Bible is of infinite value, as a witness to Christ. It can never take the place of a moral agent sanctified and filled with the Spirit, in drawing men to Christ.*

But if the Bible cannot take the place of the living teacher, neither can it take the place of the faithful pastor and guide of souls. Quackery is not in our days confined to religion. There are book-makers

---

* Christian preaching, as the living witness for Christ, as the living proclamation of the law and the Gospel, to awaken and strengthen faith, to build up the fellowship of the world, is not merely a spontaneous work of a private individual, not merely an arrangement made by the Church. It rests upon the command of Christ Himself. The command of Christ for preaching—"Go ye into all the world, and preach the Gospel to every creature" (Mark xvi. 15)—relates in the first instance to missionary work; but the newly converted ever need new instruction and edification. "If ye continue in my word (Ἐὰν ὑμεῖς μείνητε ἐν τῷ λόγῳ τῷ ἐμῷ), then are ye My disciples indeed, and ye shall

who, for the payment of a dollar, profess
to make "every man his own doctor,"
"every man his own lawyer," and "every
woman her own cook." Happily the world
has not gone altogether after them! There
are people left who still believe that medicine encounters hinderances to its working in the human subject besides mere physical disease. There are moral conditions,
peculiarities of temperament and of habit,
which need the watchful eye and the constant care of a good physician. Cookery
learned from a book is all very well for the

---

know the truth, and the truth shall make you free." (John viii. 31.)
And herein is clearly implied the appointment of preaching, as a per-
manent and constituent part of Christian worship, just as we hear
from the Apostle that the world has ordained " Pastors and Teach-
ers" in His Church, for "the perfecting of the Saints, for the
edifying of the body of Christ" (Eph. iv. 11, 12). It is not that
they are merely speakers and hearers for mutual edification, who
edify one another by the preaching of the Word ; it is the Lord
Himself who builds up His Church by the means of grace. As
the heaven-ascended Saviour, He is present with His word in the
power of His spirit. He gives to the preaching its due authority
and its proper unction; invisibly He works together with His preachers. "They went forth and preached everywhere, the Lord *working with them.*" (Mark xvi. 20).—Martensen.

honeymoon, but it will not stand the wear and tear of ordinary life. So it is also in the affairs of the soul. Jesus gave command- ment to His Apostles, not to preach only, and make disciples in His Name ; they were to play the part of shepherds to the lambs ; were to feed His sheep. They were rightly to divide the word of truth, and give to each his portion of meat in due season. Babes must be fed on milk ; strong men want meat. The Bible takes for granted an order of men to dispense it. It was given to *fix* * the oral tradition of the Church, not to take the place of the fundamental institutions which Christ her Lord had Himself established. It would be as reasonable for a sick man to substitute the reading of a book for the taking of the

---

* Neither hath He by speech only, but by writing also, instruct- ed and taught His Church. The cause of writing hath been to the end that things by him revealed unto the world might have the longer continuance, and the greater authority of assurance, by how much that standeth on record hath, in both those respects, pre- eminence above that which passeth from hand to hand, and hath no pens but the tongues, no book but the ears of men to record it. —Hooker.

medicine which a regular physician prescribed, and expect a cure, as it is for a sinner
to put the reading of God's Word in the place
of the sacraments and the prescribed means
of grace.

We now reach the πρῶτον ψεῦδος, the
prime fallacy, of modern criticism. If there
be one truth to which the Bible bears witness
more than another, it is that God has never
left men to themselves, and to the state of
nature, as it is called, to seek after Him, if
haply they might find Him. Before man
ever fell, if the Bible be true, God took man
out of the state of nature and put him into
a state of grace. When God made the
world, He did not leave the world and man
to Fortune or to blind Fate. He who made
the world for man, prepared for man a special
seat and habitation, where He revealed Himself to man by the Angel of His presence,
and entered into the communion with Him.
The world was created to be the sphere of

man's moral development. From the mo-
ment that development began, God entered
into history; and Himself took the direction
of things into His own hands. He did it in
a way, too, not to interfere with man's free
will, and sense of personal responsibility.
He bestowed His grace, not directly, but
through sacramental channels, as in the
tree of life. After creating things anew,
He withdrew Himself and made men His
ministers. If, through human weakness or
frailty, His purpose was thwarted, or His
hopes in selecting certain instruments disappointed; or His institutions through way-
wardness or wickedness perverted, still He
never abandoned the world in despair: He
modified His plan; He chose new instruments; He created new agencies; He
adapted His institutions to meet new exigencies. It has been so the ages all along for
six thousand years; it will be so, He prom-
ises us, to the end. To all this, the Bible is

the witness. It is for this we esteem it as more precious than gold of Ophir ; it is the book of books, in value and in importance, beyond all price. But how does modern criticism deal with it ? It would have us, first of all, reject, as of no value, the witness of the men who were most interested in preserving the Sacred Scriptures with scrupulous care and fidelity. It would have us believe these men knew nothing about the real value of Holy Scriptures, or the true nature of their contents. We are to believe, according to Kalisch and others, that institutions were not founded when it is said they were, because they were not at once acknowledged, and in every detail recognized, according to their value. The law, as written in the Pentateuch, could not have been given, we are told with charming simplicity, because it was not kept. The Pentateuch must belong to a later age, because its provisions were not complied with, or fully carried out, until the

time of the Babylonish captivity. Now
what is all this but to deny the very principle on which Divine Revelation goes from
the beginning to the end? It is to take a
positive Gentile and heathen notion, and to
substitute it for that which is its opposite,
and then measure things accordingly. God
indeed left the Gentiles to their own way;
He allowed them to develop as they could
their religion out their own inner conscious-
ness, to the end that they might, in time,
come to the knowledge of their ignorance,
and learn by experience their folly : but in
the case of the Jews, He gave them their
religion at the start. He planned for them
their fundamental institutions ; and He did
it with a view to educate them by presenting
to them, from the outset, an ideal which
He well knew they could never carry out in
all its fullness, or hope to attain unto as a
rule of life and conduct. Holy Scriptures
themselves bear witness in every instance, to

this failure; and they do so for the purpose
of showing how the very shortcomings of
God's ancient people were all the time bring-
ing them nearer and nearer to Him who
alone could fulfill the law in its integrity, and
make it to be, not in the letter, but in the
spirit, a rule of life. Holy Scripture, as
Archbishop Trench in his Hulsean Lectures
has well said, "*is the history of men in
a constitution—of men not seeking relations
with God, but having them, and whose task
is now to believe in them and to maintain
them.*" If this be so, then the Bible is
of no saving value without the Church. It
was written for men "not seeking relations
with God, but having them; whose task it is
now to believe in them and maintain them."
It is one of the wonders of the world, how
this fundamental truth should be written on
every page of the Bible, from the beginning
to the end, and yet so many never see it
there or take it in so as to believe in it.

III.

HOW IS THE BIBLE TO BE READ?

III.

HOW IS THE BIBLE TO BE READ?

IT is to be read as one book, and can never be divided into two. Spiritual things are to be spiritually discerned. The Old Testament is the true and only key to the New. One or two illustrations will make our meaning plain. Modern science has discovered that there is an archetypal plan in nature. There is a general plan, and there are special adaptations* all the way through. Not only is the one not opposed to the other, but the one is to some extent

* McCosh on "Typical Forms and Special Ends in Creation." Chap. II.

the outcome of the other. The fin of the fish and the wing of the bird are the homologues of the arm of the man : each is adapted to do its work in its own peculiar sphere. Nature, so to speak, tried her "'prentice hand" on the one before she attempted the other. The fish came first, the bird after, the man last, as the perfection of all—the crown and glory of all created forms. So is it in the economy of grace. Eve, when Cain was born, thought she had brought forth the Redeemer of the world; she cried in the simplicity of her faith : "I have gotten a man, the Lord." She believed in the promise, and was saved just as we are, by faith in the Lord Jesus; but her faith needed to be educated, and she had to learn by sad and painful experience that the Redeemer is to come not in the way of nature, but is to be as Seth was, " another seed," a gift of grace. Sarah learned the same lesson, but in another way. She too had faith, although she laughed when the promise at first was given, when it was long in coming. She gave Hagar to Abraham, and had a slave-born child, if not the heir of promise. She was punished for her sin, but got the child of promise at last, if not in a natural, in a supernatural way. It is the old story of Eve, but in another fashion. Look at it again : Abel was killed out of pride by a brother's hand; Isaac, the child of hope long deferred, was given by his father a sacrifice over unto death. So in latter days, one was slain out of envy, and because his spirit of meek surrender was of more value in God's sight, than works done in a spirit of pride and self-conceit. He who was thus killed by wicked hands was given over by his father a willing sacrifice unto death ; and His seed has become as the stars of heaven for multitude. Is there any possible connection between one thing and another? Read the story of Joseph

He was the child of Rachel, and came, like Isaac, after other experiments had been tried and failed, and was an answer to prayer, and a gift of grace. Joseph, too, was hated of his brethren, and was sold by them, and was given over unto death. But he came out of the pit, and was lifted from a prison to the throne, and was made lord over the whole land of Egypt; and the command was given that every knee should bow before him. It is the same fundamental type, but with variations and new adaptations. Can it have any reference to One who in after times was hated of his brethren, and was sold, and was taken from the pit and the prison-house to be lord and ruler over all, to whom every knee is to bow and every tongue confess that He is Lord to the glory of God the Father?

But we are in a new sphere, and a new order is round about us. The old covenant was established in a trinity of persons, who held peculiar relations one to the other. Abraham was the high father, who through his only begotten and well beloved son, became, by faith, the father of many nations. Isaac was the incarnation of meekness, and obedience itself; and Jacob was a supplanter and a wrestler with God, a builder of houses consecrated to worship, and the head of the twelve tribes of Israel. Is it more than possible that we have foreshadowed here another and a better covenant? Do we see the beginning of the adjustment of the relations of another Trinity; have intimations given of another Wrestler and Supplanter; note the coming of another Builder and Consecrator; and are made to anticipate the Progenitor of another twelve and seventy, in ages yet to come? And if so, why does God take this way of preparing the world's "gray fathers" for the advent of the world's Redeemer? The possible solution of the mystery is that these ancient patriarchs, in the simplicity

of their faith, and their feebleness of spiritual apprehension, were after all but beginners
in a training-school. These pictures which
pass before us with all their wonderful sim-
ilarity in diversity, repeating the story over
and over again with adaptations and constant
filling in, were after all like our own *Kinder-
garten* object lessons, where sense apprehends
by means of the eye, and touch, and use,
the things which the logical faculty and
the spiritual powers of the soul, when fully
developed, are to grasp in the form of supernatural truth. Christ and His Church are
the development and growth of the Old
Testament and its history, just as man and
nature are the growth of centuries, and were
seen in archetypal light long before the
world as it now is appeared. If it be the
work of the true philosopher, as Lord Bacon
says, to interpret nature, it is none the less
the work of the theologian to trace the plan
hidden in the Old Testament from stage to

stage, and show its completion and fulfillment in the New. It may safely be affirmed that no system of theology is worth a fig which does not accept as a fundamental maxim that spiritual things are to be spiritually discerned, and makes use of the things of the Old Testament as object lessons, to unlock the mysteries of the New.

The Bible, to be read with profit, must be read in the order in which it is arranged in the Canon, and not according to any system of chronology, or natural selection. The law as given in the Pentateuch is the basis of the whole revelation, but it is not as the Samaritans or the Sadducees held, the whole of revelation. The Law is supplemented by the Prophets as the objective by subjective, the factual (if we may be allowed the word) and institutional by the critical and the progressive. If we were to judge of the condition of any country by the morning papers, we should think the world was drawing near its

3*

close.   The liberty of the press is a priceless
heritage, although it does not always measure with exactness of speech the evils it seeks
to correct.   So with the Prophets ; they were
sent to enforce the great and all-important
truth that God looks for more than outward
service ; He expects purity of heart, as well as
purity of hands and feet.   No gift is of any
value to Him where the giver is not one with
the offering.   Priest and king have no honor
save as they represent Him, and use the
power committed to them for the good of
those for whom it was given.   These are
surely eternal, imperishable truths ; they are
the truths which Wicklif and Hus preached
in modern times ; but they are perverted
when it is forgotten that it is against the
abuse and not against the use of the things
contained in the law they are directed.   God
cannot contradict Himself ; what He doeth
He doeth it forever.   The Law, the Priest-
hood, the Altar, Sacrificial Ordinances—

Kings, Judges, Rulers—are all the ordinance
of God and are to be obeyed as His ; they are
all, however, means to an end, and that end is
one, though double in its working, viz., the
good of the creature and the glory of the
Creator.*

The Hagiographa, in contradistinction to
the law and the prophets, is mystical and spiritual in its application. Here the ordinary
economic conditions which are of force in the
earlier stages of the Divine life are swallowed
up of the supernatural and the eternal. The
mighty stream of the Church's devotional and

---

* " While the calling of the priest seeks to realize the letter of the
law, that of the prophet endeavors to realize its spirit. The prophets in general demand obedience to God's will as revealed in His
laws, and are fond of emphasizing the pre-Mosaic and decalogue
command respecting the observance of the Sabbath ; but Malachi's
censure with reference to the malobservance of the sacrificial Tôrah
(i. 10, etc.) stands absolute and alone. In every case the exhorta-
tions of the prophets do not refer to the externals, but to the substance of the law. They are zealous against the heartless and
spiritless *opus operatum* of dead works. With biting sarcasm they
depreciate ceremonial observance and fasting (Hosea vi. 6;
Jeremiah vii. 21–23 ; Joel ii. 13 ; Isaiah lviii). In brief the priest
is the guardian of the external letter of the law, and the prophet of
the internal, spiritual fulfillment."—Delitzsch.

spiritual life broadens and ripens, until it embraces Gentile as well as Jew; and breaks away beyond the barriers of time, and space, and economic dispensation, carrying along with it all that is richest and best in the experience of devout souls in every country and of every kind.*

* "The tendency of the age of Solomon in relation to the tendency of that of David, may be compared to the tendency of Alexandrian Judaism, in relation to that of the Palestinian. It is directed to the human, the ideal, and the universal elements in Israel's religion and history, and connects the essence of the Israelitish religion with the elements of truth in heathenism. As knowledge (*gnosis*) goes forth from faith (*pistis*) so the age of Solomon is the new age of wisdom (*chokma*) which has gone forth from David. While prophecy serves the process of redemptive history, chokma hastens before it and anticipates the universal ideas, through which the adaptation of the religion of Jehovah to become the religion of the world is recognized."—Delitzsch.

To the same purport Godet says: "It is beyond dispute that, under the influence of the genius of Solomon, there grew up in his court a school of *wisdom*, or of moral philosophy, and that this phenomenon was in Israel a fact of an altogether new kind. Whilst the Levitical institutions performed their functions regularly, and the Mosaic ordinances were more and more impressing their stamp upon the life of the people, the leading minds, with the King Himself at their head, were feeling the necessity of searching more deeply into the knowledge of things, divine and human. Beneath the Israelite, they tried to find the man; beneath the Mosaic system, that universal principle of the moral law, of which it is the perfect expression. Then they

If we would read the New Testament with
profit, we must remember at the outset that
the Gospel is to be sought for not in any one
Gospel, but in all the four Gospels combined.
We have four differing, but not contra-
dictory, aspects of our Lord's life presented
for consideration. We view the mystery of
His Divine-human personality on all its four
sides, as a complete manifestation of Godhead, through the medium of humanity to
the whole world. We see Him first, as the
Jews thought about Him and looked for
Him. We see Him again as the Romans
received Him, not so much as a Teacher as
an Actor, and the Founder of a universal
kingdom in the world. We see Him again

reached to that idea of *wisdom* which is the common feature of the
three books, Proverbs, Job, and Ecclesiastes. The Divine wisdom
in the idea of which are included the notions of intelligence, jus-
tice, and goodness, is personified as the supreme object of Divine
love, and as the spirit which gives existence and order to the
world ; this wisdom has marked with her stamp everything in the
universe ; her delight is not in the Jews only, but in the *children
of men.* To conform to her laws, is for man wisdom ; to act
against them folly."

in His relationship to the world at large, and
to the outcast sinners of the Gentiles, the
Seeker of the lost, and the Healer of the sick,
and the Provider of an inn for the wayfarers
spoiled and robbed by the wayside.   Last of
all, we see Him as the Eternal Archetype,
the Light that lighteth every man that cometh
into the world, taking humanity into union
with Divinity, that He might, by entering
into the conditions of time and mortality, fill
it with the fullness of His own uncreated
and eternal life.

Like the Law in the old dispensation, the
Gospel is only the beginning, not the end
of all that Jesus began both to do and to
teach.   Here we see Him creating and calling into being things that were not.   In the
Acts of the Apostles we see Him from His
eternal throne, operating in and through His
Church; and by virtue of the unction bestowed upon Him in return for His finished
works, doing greater works than any which

in His own Person He had done while here
upon the earth. The Acts supplement the
Gospels. Here we see fulfilled what was
promised there. Jesus came not to make
disciples only, but to found and establish
a kingdom also. Now we see Him as a
King upon His throne, and witness in the
new spirit infused into the Apostles the
secret of the power that has made the
Church triumphant over the world. The
Epistles are as many-sided as the Gospels.
Here, Peter and John and James apply the
lessons learned of Jesus in their familiar
intercourse with Him for the guidance and
instruction of the Church. Paul, as one born
out of due time, arises to meet the wants
of the Church when it overleaped the bound-
aries of Jerusalem and the Holy Land,
and began to embrace the Gentiles within
its bosom. The whole is crowned with the
Book of the Revelation where "the heaven
which had disappeared from the earth

since the third chapter of Genesis re-appears again in visible manifestation. The tree of life, whereof there were but faint reminiscences all the intermediate time, again stands by the river of the water of life, and again there is no more curse. Even the very differences of the forms under which the heavenly kingdom re-appears are doubly characteristic, marking as they do not merely all that is won back, but won back in a more glorious shape than that in which it was lost, because won back by the Son. It is no longer Paradise, but the New Jerusalem—no longer the *Garden*, but now the *City* of God, which is on earth. The change is full of meaning: no longer the garden, free, spontaneous, and unlabored, even as man's blessedness in the first estate of innocence would have been ; but the City, costlier indeed, more stately, more glorious, but at the same time the result of toil, of labor, of pains—reared into a nobler and more abiding habitation, yet with stones which, after the pattern of the 'elect corner stone,' were each, in its turn, laboriously hewn and painfully squared for the places which they fill." *

It will be seen that the Bible is not only one book as the revelation of God's eternal plan, but is likewise a complete and organic whole in which part is dovetailed, by an all-pervading law of spiritual growth and development, into part. The Old Testament is the preparation for the New, and the New is the fulfilling of the Old. What if there be ten thousand times ten thousand various readings; what if through "redactions" and adjustments for ecclesiastical purposes, parts have been transposed, or additions here and there made; what if St. Paul did not write the Epistle to the Hebrews; let ingenuity and perverse criticism twist and turn things as they may, these are but scratches on the surface of a Book which, the more one reads

* Trench.

it, the more they stand amazed at its awful depth, and are at times ready to fall prostrate in the presence of the all-informing Spirit Who there reveals to those who have the eyes to see the workings of God's eternal plan.

The Bible, moreover, is its own best interpreter. One of the coming devises of the later criticism is to compare the Bible with other (so called) scriptures, and in this way try to rob it of everything like a peculiarly distinctive character. Lenormant furnishes us with " The Beginnings of History according to the Bible and the Traditions of Oriental Peoples from the Creation of Man to the Deluge," and another treats us to "The Sacred Scriptures of the World," etc., etc.* Now, it is to be granted that the Bible has much in common with other books, whether sacred or profane ; it is to be maintained, notwithstanding that the Bible is a book *sui generis*, and from the

---

* See an able review of "Sacred Scriptures of the World," etc., in the *Am. Lit. Churchman*, for May 1, 1883.

beginning to the end, follows a purpose and a plan peculiarly its own. Other books and other religions have accounts of the creation of the world, as well as the Bible; but there is in the Biblical account a something which is not to be found in any. It was the *universal* belief of the ancient world that matter is eternal. The Bible, on the other hand, affirms that God called the matter of the world into being, as well as gave to everything that exists its peculiar form. The first chapter of Genesis and the first article of the Creed are in perfect harmony one with another. It is also peculiar to the Bible that it speaks of God as creating all things by His word, and through the in-breathing of His Holy Spirit. This is an idea that pervades all Holy Scriptures, and is as true of the New Creation in Christ Jesus, as it is of the Old Creation of which the first Adam was the crown. It is also peculiar to the Biblical story that the account of the nat-

ural creation is only the introduction to a
series of productions or origins, in which God
appears, not as the Maker of the world only,
but as a Person who lives and moves in history, and holds personal communion and fellowship with the sons of men.   The Book of
Genesis is not, as its title would at first seem
to indicate, a mere account of the creation
of the world, but is made up of ten *toledoths*,
or successions of creative acts in which God
is represented as laying in the world the
foundations of an eternal plan, which is to
find its consummation at the last in the incarnation of His own Eternal Son, and in the
establishment of a kingdom that is to endure
forever.   It is not in vain, then, that the account of the first creation is repeated in a
second and supplementary chapter of this
same book of Genesis.   The heavens and
the earth do not exist for themselves ; they
were not intended only to display the glory
of their Creator ; they were created to be the

sphere of the moral development of the human race ; and of the union of God and man
in connection with it.   It is for this reason
man made with a mere distinction of sex
in the first chapter of Genesis, appears in the
form of a twofold personality in the second.
It is for the same reason Elohim, the sum
and source of all power, the world's great
First Cause, is represented under a personal
name, Jehovah, and condescends to talk with
man as friend with friend, face to face. This
idea of a twofold relationship of God to
man, and of man to God, is an idea which
runs throughout all Holy Scripture, from
first to last, and is peculiar to itself.   It is
not to be accounted for by a theory like that
of Astruc (known as the document-hypothe-
sis), but by the fact that man on his earthly
side is part and parcel of nature, and is gov-
erned by the law of cause and effect accordingly, while on his heavenly side he
is, by the fact of his personality and free

agency, lifted above all earthly powers, and
made capable of entering into communion
and fellowship with the eternal I AM. The as-
sertion, then, that in the twofold account of
the creation, given in the first and second
chapters of Genesis, we have *one* representa-
tion, made up out of two separate and con-
tradictory sets of documents (as asserted by
the rationalistic school), is seen to be at variance with the whole drift of Divine Revelation. The notion that any man, gifted with
common sense, could deliberately sit down
to compile a history from two sets of documents at variance, one with the other, and
call it a revelation from God, is simply too
monstrous for rational belief, and yet it is this
that we are asked to receive at the hands of
the later criticism.

Again we are told that every mythology
has its golden age, just as the Bible has its
story of Paradise and the age of innocence.
There is enough in the statement to catch

the unwary, especially when served up with
a show of learning about Kritayuga, "the
age of perfection," and Dvparayuga, "the
age of doubt," and Kaliyuga, "the age of
"perdition," as in the Aryan tradition. But
the correspondence here, as elsewhere, is
only on the surface. The Biblical idea of
Paradise, as it appears in the Jehovistic
account of the Creation, is essentially a *sacramental* idea, and not a state of nature at
all. The Bible, in other words, represents
the state of nature, described in the first
chapter of the Book of Genesis, as a state
not *natural* to man, but to the lower creatures; out of which man was, was taken
by a special act of grace, and was placed
amid moral relationships, and was sur-
rounded with sacramental signs and symbols
which were intended to have an educational
effect upon him. The lower creatures are
allowed to have indiscriminate concubin-
age one with another; man is not. The

brute creation may eat of everything to
the full; man must place a restraint on
appetite if he will raise himself to partici-
pation in a higher life. It is from this point,
history takes its start, and why? Because
man in the state of nature has no history.
He must subject himself to moral conditions
before history can begin. History begins
after the moral struggle which marks the
epoch of the fall. Now all this again is
peculiar to Holy Scriptures; it is part and
parcel, moreover, of a class of ideas which
have here their germ, and which continue
to germinate and develop through all suc-
ceeding dispensations to the close of the
Book of Revelation.

It will be seen, at a glance, that in
this twofold account of the creation of man,
and of the relation which God bears to him,
in the one state or in the other, we have the
foundation laid for the later division of the
human family into Jews and Gentiles; and

4

the determination of the Divine relations accordingly. The Gentiles represent that portion of the race which fall away into the state of nature, and worship the powers of nature, and are debased as a consequence thereof ; the Jews are those who exist in a state of separation from the world, and worship, not the God of Nature, but the personal Jehovah, who manifests Himself by the angel of His presence to them. They abhor fornication, and keep with religious exactness the unity of the marriage bond (as an ideal at least) ; they perpetuate in the world the idea of a God who is separate from nature ; and Who speaks to men by the agency of His word, and educates them by the instrumentality of His Holy Spirit. If it be true, then, that the Bible has some things in common with other religions, and with other books ; it is also true that it moves in a circle of ideas peculiarly its own. If we would read and study it aright, we must make it our aim, not so much to search out what it has in common with other Scriptures, but strive to grasp the ideas, which give to it its own peculiar character, and on which it founds its claims to be, as no other book can be, a revelation of God from Heaven.

Among other attempts made at the present time to degrade the Bible and to rob it of its distinctive character, is one even more Jesuitical (for Rationalism has its Jesuits as well as Rome) than that to which attention has just been called. It is proposed to expurgate the Bible after the fashion of the ancient *classics*, as containing things which are offensive to polite ears, and positively hurtful to good morals. The proposition is as monstrous as it is destructive of the very fundamental idea of Divine Revelation. One great object for which Holy Scriptures were given was to bear witness against the world's sin. The Christian Church from the beginning has

used Holy Scriptures in three ways, chiefly. It
has been her custom to read Holy Scripture
publicly in the congregation, that she may
thereby, in her prophetical character, bear
continual witness against the world's sin.
The Anglican Church, accordingly, does not
permit her clergy to select what they shall
read, lest they should cease to bear witness
against prevailing forms of error ; but makes
it her aim to read the whole Sacred Volume
(as far as possible) through, year by year, in
order that her children may have before them
continually the whole counsel of God. In ad-
dition to this, she has her liturgical or devotional use of Holy Scriptures in the office for
the Holy Communion. The liturgical use
for devotional purposes is no substitute for
the prophetical as a witness against the
world's sin, but is supplementary to it. Then,
in the textual use of Scripture, we have the
application of the substance of the Divine
Revelation to the wants of the individual :

an application still more extended in its homiletical or expository use. An expurgated Bible means neither more nor less than an attempt to divide and kill the prophets, as they did of old time, lest they should any longer bear witness against the evil that is in the world.

There are two vulgar errors continually to be met with (even among devout persons) in the reading of the Bible, against which, in conclusion, we would give a word of warning. It is not the case that a text, or saying, or argument is inspired, because it is found in the Bible. Balaam was a false prophet, and he gave utterance to many elevated sentiments, as, for example, "let me die the death of the righteous, and let my last end be like his," but we are not on that account to think that all Balaam said and did was the result of Divine inspiration. The same is true of Job's friends; they were "miserable counsellors," albeit they spoke much that was

true, and good for Job to hear. It is no
uncommon thing, it has been observed, for
preachers to take a text, or quote in support
of some doctrine, or some position, the
words or the actions of men, simply because
they occur in Scripture, treating all as equally
inspired, because the book from which they
quote is written by an inspired man ; or as
the statement is commonly made, it is found
in the inspired Word of God. Jeremy Tay-
lor, in one of his most beautiful sermons,—
that preached at the funeral of the Countess
of Carberry,—takes for his text the words
of the woman of Tekoah, 2 Sam. xiv. 14,
which he uses throughout, as if they were the
words of one speaking by the spirit of God.
Perhaps no passage is more frequently used
in this way than one spoken by the Pharisees
against our Lord, and his Divine power, at
a time when our Lord worked a miracle, and
used a form of words in working it, for the
very purpose of refuting the doctrine which

these words express. Our Lord in healing a certain paralytic, said, " Man, thy sins are forgiven thee." The Pharisees murmured at this, and exclaimed that such a form was blasphemy, for, "who can forgive sins but God only?" Our Lord replied, that He used that form purposely to show them that "the Son of Man hath power on earth to forgive sins." It is very common now to hear persons quote these words of the Pharisees, to show that the Bible denies that Christ has given power to his ministers to pronounce absolution, or at least that they have power to forgive sins. Such persons might quote, as equally taught by the Bible, that our Lord was a Samaritan and had a devil, for it was the same persons, the Pharisees, that said it of him." St. Paul warns us that even among inspired men there are things spoken by " authority," and things which are spoken only in the way of advice.* In the

* 1 Cor. vii, 25.

one case there is a law of perpetual obligation to be observed; in the other the injunction was temporary, and given to meet "the present distress."

Again in reading Holy Scriptures it is dangerous to trust to isolated texts. It is ever to be remembered, as well for the defence as for the confirmation of the faith, that it is the spirit, not the letter of Holy Scriptures that is to be our guide. We have a notable instance of this in the way the Old Testament is quoted in the New. There would seem in some cases to be a positive disregard of the letter, and that, too, with a view, it would seem, of preserving the spirit in the transfer of the passage from its application under the old economy to the things of the new dispensation. It matters really nothing, so far as the doctrine of the Trinity is concerned, whether (in 1. Tim. iii. 16) the true rendering of the oldest MSS. be O or Θ. The faith of the Church does not depend upon such an uncertain issue as the carelessness of a scribe or the legibility of a manuscript." Verbal criticism may do its work, and still no essential dogma be imperiled or impinged upon. " Scripture interpretation, it has been said, should be comprehensive as well as exact and literal. We must weigh one part against another ; we must give to each phrase its broader rather than its narrower meaning ; we must take the tenor of the faith for our guidance, if we would enter into the mind of the Spirit."